Reflective Awareness

Experience Life to the Fullest

Elizabeth Cook

Deep Breaths, Elizabeth Cook

Speak It To Book
www.speakittobook.com

Reflective Awareness / Elizabeth Cook
ISBN-13: 978-1-945793-82-0

To Dad—the man who has always been my wisdom teacher, continues to guide me through this journey we call life, and reminds me daily to be humble.

To Mom—the woman who gave me my confidence, always made the small moments magical when I was a child, and continues to show me how to capture those moments each day.

CONTENTS

A Fulfilling Life

My mother made magic from the mundane. While many of my peers' fondest childhood memories are of vacations and extraordinary events, mine are of walks to the park, sitting silently in the forest, and watching sunsets in the backyard. My mother made these moments memorable and special, and her unique perspective of considering every moment as a gift has shaped me into the woman I am today.

Many of us mothers want to communicate the preciousness of the present moment to our children. We want to show them the beauty of small moments so they can better appreciate the life they've been given—so they can become who they were meant to be. And yet those moments seem to bury us.

Work, school, schedules, appointments, to-do lists that extend until the end of time—we're so busy and stretched thin that we fail to make the most of every moment. We show up to work but never give it our all. We pursue a college degree, but only halfheartedly. We're home for dinner and yet we're not fully present.

If we're not living at our best, then what message does that give to our employers, our spouse, our children?

My Story

I was born and raised in Pittsburgh, Pennsylvania. I was the youngest of three and the baby girl to our family. My father was a CFO of a Fortune 500 company, and my mother was a nurse. They both worked throughout my childhood.

My parents and my two older brothers were, and continue to be, my rocks. I would even call my brothers my best friends. I loved school from an early age; I was the only sibling my parents enrolled in preschool, as my mom told me I was trying to do my brothers' homework from a very early age. I was athletic and loved to be outside in nature. I found my childhood friends early in my school years, and they continue to be my friends today.

My dad always believed in me and helped guide me. I fondly remember him taking me to a construction site when I was twelve years old. Dad pointed to a group of men with construction boots and hard hats and stated, "If you get your engineering degree, you can be the boss of this big site." I don't remember me wanting to be a boss, but I do remember the sincerity of my dad telling me I could be whatever I wanted. As my brothers and I grew older, he would frequently remind us that being an engineer was the way to go and that it would provide us with a degree that would open doors and pay the bills.

My brothers and I all became engineers. High school

has been the most challenging part of my life thus far. I was studious and athletic, but, as many have told me, I was an old soul and wanted to graduate before my time. I started working my first job when I was fifteen as a lifeguard and worked in fast food as well. When I had the opportunity, I worked two jobs. Social atmospheres made me feel lonely and isolated, so I found comfort in work. I was very independent from an early age.

After graduating from high school, I initially enrolled in the engineering program at Pennsylvania State University. After one year, however, I was homesick and transferred to the University of Pittsburgh, where I commuted from home. The majority of my classes were filled almost entirely with men, with only one or two women, though I didn't even recognize it at the time or think of myself as the minority. It wasn't until we took our graduation picture that I realized I was the only woman out of forty graduating with a bachelor's degree in electrical engineering that year.

I believe I was able to face challenges and obstacles with gusto because my dad told me I could be anything I put my mind to and because my mom instilled me with confidence. I loved every minute of my college experience. It was not typical though, as I spent long days on campus five days a week attending classes and working on schoolwork with my peers and then worked as a bartender forty hours a week Thursday through Sunday. I loved to be busy, and the job gave me the social environment my heart desired.

I met my husband when I was twenty-one and had recently graduated from college while bartending. I was planning to attend graduate school at the University of Pittsburgh in the fall of that year, however I accepted a corporate job that would pay for my master's degree. He took me on a date to celebrate my first day at my new job. Soon after starting my career, we married and I adopted his three-year-old daughter, whose mother had passed away prior to our introduction. My friends and family expressed concern when I took on all these new responsibilities. How could I possibly balance a career and a family at such a young age?

Maybe it was my mother's example that gave me the confidence, but never for a moment did I doubt myself. I knew I could create a plan, and I knew I could succeed. I embraced my family network, and I accepted their help. I made a point to be fully present with my family when I was with them and also fully present at work during work hours. Consequently, my career grew—and so did my family!

Now, at 36, I am a senior manager of an engineering program and am working on my doctorate. I'm also a graduate of the Institute for Integrative Nutrition, where I learned innovative coaching methods, practical lifestyle management techniques, and everything in between regarding the power of mindset and being a self-advocate for my health.

I have six beautiful children, ages 18 down to 1, and we are thriving. My family has all of me, and so does my career. Sure, there is always a stack of dishes to be washed, but there are plenty of hands to help.

Pursuing my passions has allowed me to create the best environment for success. I've never used my children as a reason for not delivering or showing up. I'm a high performer, always motivated, always positive. The key is balance. Knowing when to work from home. Knowing how to juggle schedules. Knowing when it's time for self-care, time with friends, or moments of quiet.

I firmly believe these things are possible for anyone who is willing to put in the effort, and that's why I'm writing this book.

The Beauty of Mindfulness

A close friend of mine has two kids and works. She's frazzled—and understandably so. That's a lot to take on. She constantly says she does not have time for the things she wants to do most. Her biggest dreams, ambitions, and even hobbies are being set aside as she tries to get through the day.

Perhaps you feel like my friend. I'm sure we all have felt overwhelmed and frazzled, but I'm here to encourage you to step back and analyze how you spend your time. Instead of allowing the hustle and bustle to rule the day, we need to stop. We need a plan. We need to structure our lives so that we can be present for all that we have in front of us.

My hope for you, as you read this book, is that you can live a fulfilling life while juggling career and family or whatever your commitments may be. While there is no clear definition anywhere for how to be a "perfect" mom, there is a lot of talk about expectations and best practices as a parent. But you don't have to be anything; you are who you are. Realizing that, we can then be mindful of our thoughts and emotions when we are confronted with various circumstances.

To get to and cultivate a place of mindfulness, we can practice three techniques that will help us experience life to the fullest:

Carve out and structure your day to include "you time." This is your time to be quiet and alone with your thoughts, because you must take care of yourself before you can take care of others.

Meditate daily. Try to be still for ten minutes with your thoughts and then journal them. If possible, organize your thoughts into action steps.

Recognize that feelings and thoughts drive your actions. Your thoughts will breed emotions, both good and bad. Be aware of how this can affect your choices, your attitude, and your performance.

These techniques for mindfulness encourage us to channel our thoughts whenever we don't feel like doing something, even though we know we need to do it.

When we can be mindful of what we are doing, even though we'd rather not, it empowers us on the inside in a way that we may not have realized was possible. From there, we can realize our potential as we take control of thoughts and move forward in an intentional, positive way. Mindfulness helps us put our actions into place.

But as we chase after mindfulness, there are obstacles to be wary of:

Fear of failure. The risk of failing in front of everyone is one of the biggest fears that people face. Fear will stop your development before it starts, and it will keep you where you've always been—living a life that is stressful, chaotic, and a far cry from what it could be.

Lack of self-belief. The reason you are stuck in life is because you have believed the lies that say you're not smart enough, you're not skilled enough, you're not important enough, or you're not liked enough.

Problems with finances. Money is one of life's biggest stresses. If you're not mindful of your finances, it can wreak havoc on your mindset and put you in a state of constant panic and worry, whether you're making six figures or minimum wage.

Impact from negative people who do not allow change. Negative people steal the positivity and joy from what you're trying to do. They can be your parents, friends, or even your significant other.

Ready, Set, Go!

Life can be full, and you can achieve everything you want to achieve—no compromise, no end-of-the-day exhaustion. Your thoughts and feelings create action. You decide your life. Fear and stress will try to hold you back, but I'm here to tell you that things can change, and this book will show you how. It will equip you to change your interior life in a way that impacts your exterior life. At the end of each chapter, workbook sections will help you activate this transformation in your life.

It starts with you. Start now by asking yourself, "What do I want to do or accomplish in a day, week, month, or year?" "What drives me to get up in the morning?"

This book will help provide a path for you to get there. It will bring mindfulness and will empower you to live a life that is balanced, so that you can accomplish all that is on your plate.

CHAPTER ONE

Emotional Awareness

My dad had a unique perspective on raising me. When I turned two years old, he began treating me like a little adult. He gave me options. Did I want to wear my green shirt or purple shirt? Did I want to play with blocks or puzzles? Did I want to go with him to the store or stay home?

It sounds simple, but this technique allowed me to manage my emotions. I realized that I had some control over my life, and my voice mattered. I realized that I could choose my path.

Many people do not come to this realization, even in adulthood. They believe that life is the way that it is and there's no changing it. They feel trapped and locked in. And they've never progressed emotionally from that childhood state of helplessness. The norm for women is to feel overwhelmed, overbook themselves, and suffer from sleep deprivation, leaving them without the time or energy to make good, healthy decisions. We feel underappreciated, and we don't know how to get out from under the weight.

Dr. Daniel Siegel's book *The Whole-Brain Child* thoroughly explores the development of the brain.[1] In it, Seigel explains that babies do not realize they are entities until they are about a year old. At age 2, they are beginning to realize their emotions, but they don't know how to manage them. And yet, those emotions are real. This is why toddlers have tantrums. Essentially, as we grow, we need to work through our thoughts and emotions to get to a healthier place.

My dad always understood this.

If I was upset or crying, he asked if I wanted his help processing things. I remember many times in my childhood and adolescence when he sat with me in those chaotic, emotional moments. He didn't allow me to attach anything to that emotion.

Instead of blaming someone for why I was sad—maybe my coach was unfair or my friend had stabbed me in the back—Dad walked me through what I was feeling. He helped me embrace the fact that I could be sad without taking my coach or best friend down with me.

Some may not have been as fortunate to have a parent teach them how to manage their emotions. They are stuck being "fine" or just "okay," unable to process what's going on. Or perhaps they are angry all the time. But being able to explore all your emotions and be present in them is key to personal growth. It's a foundation toward higher-level emotional maturity.

Working Through Emotions

In the ninth grade, I was on a varsity sports team and being primed for a starting position the following year. Everything pointed to me clinching this spot for my tenth-grade year. But things didn't work out the way I expected. One of my eighth-grade teammates, a girl who was a year younger than I, quickly improved. She got so good that she ousted me from what I had assumed would be a sure position. I became a second-string benchwarmer. Of course this was very hard for me to take. Up to that point, I had been the star athlete. And in a moment, it was all taken away. I got upset on the car rides home. I complained about my coach, called him a jerk, and said he didn't know how to properly build a team.

My dad, in his wisdom, brought me through. He had me focus on my emotion rather than on the people involved. He coached me away from blaming others for how I felt. Because of him, I was able to feel my emotions and deal solely with them without casting blame.

My dad and I used to run together. I initially hated running, but I really liked being with my dad. When we ran, he coached me through the feeling of wanting to quit. If I slowed down to walk, he asked, "What made you stop running?" I told him, and he pushed for more explanation. He explored the physical aspects of why I had stopped running. Was it a lack of breath? Feeling tired? He helped me see that I was working hard, and despite feeling out of breath or tired, I actually liked the physical activity of running. To this day, I still like to run.

When I was at school studying engineering, I broke

down crying in the hallway one day. The only reason I had gone to engineering school was because my dad believed his children should have a job that would pay for their adult lives.

Frustrated, I called him and complained. I couldn't see how engineering school made sense for me. He saw through my emotion. He knew I was overwhelmed by the moment and by the rigors of school, and he knew I needed to learn to deal with that pressure and move through it— not run from it. After our conversation, I persisted and ultimately did well in school, even though it was difficult and occasionally overwhelming.

One of the best techniques my dad used to help me learn to deal with pressure and my emotions was to walk me through a calm-down process. It started with relaxing my toes. Bit by bit, I moved up my body, relaxing every part. He had me imagine blood flowing through my veins; he had me think about my heartbeat. In a way, it was a form of meditation that calmed my mind and allowed me to simply sit with my feelings. He always helped me to feel my feelings and work through them, instead of passing blame or finding a way out.

After I got married and had a baby, I needed this technique more than ever. My husband worked five nights per week, and there were times I felt alone and hopeless. I wondered what I had gotten into. *"How did I think I could do it all on my own?"*

Those feeling of being overwhelmed paralyzed me, but my dad's teachings and methods got me through those difficult moments and continue to be vital today for the management of my emotions.

Handling Emotions

I've taken my dad's teachings for handling emotions and broken them down into four steps:

Be aware of how your emotion builds. You need to be able to identify when your emotions are welling up. Maybe you become terse with others. Maybe you distance yourself. Maybe you pick your nails or eat ice cream.

Choose to deal with those emotions. Once you feel your emotions building, choose to sit in them instead of running from them or implementing coping mechanisms. Don't bury them. Think through why you're feeling what you're feeling.

Come to a place of acceptance. It's okay to feel. It's okay to be sad, mad, frustrated, hurt, or any other emotion you encounter.

Take action. Determine if you need to do anything about the emotions you're feeling. If you're frustrated with a friend, perhaps you need to go to her. If you're stressed, perhaps you need to take a day off.

This then begs the question, are there bad emotions? If I am to welcome my emotions and work through them, is there a possibility that particular emotions will harm me? What about rage? Hate? Envy?

Emotions aren't bad, but failing to explore them—and choosing instead to ignore them or deaden them—is bad.

When we think of bad emotions, we might be thinking about someone who is suppressing deep emotion therefore causing dangerous emotions to emerge. Strong, negative emotions are formed when we bury our emotions and then allow those emotions to rule.

Burying our emotions causes us to be short-tempered and slightly angry. We feel as if the world is acting against us and we don't have control over anything, which only increases our anger.

Bad emotions can also result from pampering or coddling—a tendency parents can easily fall into, resulting in children growing up not knowing how to properly handle how they're feeling. Coddling children encourages pampering of emotions, rather than releasing of emotions. For instance, when babies fall and are then showered with attention, they may start to believe that they must be hurt, sad, or screaming to get the attention they need. When these children become adults and feel sadness, they are not equipped to process and manage their emotions as mature adults. Emotionally coddled children are trained to be dependent, anxious, and fearful, instead of empowered.

Helping Children Manage Their Emotions

Children's tantrums are physical manifestations of some serious emotions going on inside. They don't know how to express themselves, and so they act out.

There are generally two approaches to managing children who are throwing tantrums. Some people baby them, pamper them, and protect them from the world. By contrast, others will tell a child, "Knock it off. Don't be that way. You're being a brat."

However, neither approach fosters a healthy relationship with emotion. When we see that a child is struggling, it's our job as adults to teach that it's okay to feel what the child is feeling. It's okay to be angry because they didn't get that gummy bear or to feel frustration because their stack of blocks tipped over.

There are several steps parents and adults can set in place to help children work through their emotions, and the steps are very close to the steps we as adults should be taking to deal with our own emotions.

Step 1: Allow children to see that feelings are legitimate. Ignoring their emotions only stifles their own personal and mental growth. Teaching them that their feelings are indeed legitimate helps them to be empathetic.

Step 2: Encourage them to handle a particular feeling appropriately with two action steps: feel it and understand it. If we don't teach our children to feel and understand their emotions, they will not be able to grow and mature.

Step 3: Help them move on. Because you have helped them process and work through their emotions, they don't need to dwell on them. They can move on in freedom and confidence.

Let me give you a practical example of this involving two of my children who share a bedroom. They often find themselves squabbling over their different opinions of what is rude and what is not rude.

When one sibling hurts the other's feelings and the argument escalates, I find myself stepping in and talking them through the incident. I allow each one of them to express their point of view, provide confirmation that their feelings and emotions are understood—not the lashing out and violence aspects, but rather, the emotions of being frustrated with each other. They each have the opportunity to speak about the incident and about how it made them feel, so they feel heard.

In helping our children through these situations, we must not make broad generalizations about them and label them as bossy, controlling, angry, immature, sensitive, etc. When we label people—especially children—and create an environment in which they cannot connect with a range of emotions in a helpful forum, we hinder them from believing in themselves.

It is also important to provide an environment where we ourselves are safe to express our feelings and thoughts—so we can develop the skills needed to express feelings appropriately in our adult lives and model those skills for our children.

Developing Emotional Awareness

When it comes to learning how to develop emotional awareness for yourself and to teaching your children and your network the same, there are certain steps to take to make this process as smooth as possible.

First, when you recognize you're experiencing a particularly tough moment (or have just experienced such a moment), ask yourself, "Why am I feeling or acting this way?" Maybe you've lost your cool with your child. Maybe you've had a post-work meltdown. Second, as you reflect on that question, put your response on paper as soon as possible. Think about what happened before you lost your cool, what happened while you lost it, and the emotions you experienced. Third, continue the process as many times as needed until you have fully worked through and processed the situation. Fourth, be mindful of your thoughts and feelings throughout the day. For this process to become second nature to you, you have to be mindful of it. Check in with yourself throughout the day. Figure out how you're doing. Eventually, when you realize you are getting upset, you'll be able to walk away from whatever situation you are in.

As you process your thoughts, you will learn to simply be present and keenly aware of your blood pressure or your heart beating or your core temperature, so that you can manage how you are feeling in tough or uncomfortable situations.

Recruit others to step in when you need help managing your emotions. For instance, my husband knew when to step in when I was mismanaging a conflict with our children. To distract me from the debates I had with them, he would ask me if I wanted chocolate cake. The goal was to get my mind out of the discussion when he could see that I was engaging with them in a way that wasn't helpful. His engagement with me helped me to stop engaging on my children's level and to refocus my own emotions and thoughts.

Once distracted, I could take a deep breath and become aware of where I was and what I was doing. I could work with my children through the conversation, and then we could move on. Most of our conversations ended with them saying, "Thank you," or "You were so right." Because I, as the parent, was calm and focused through the conversation, things could be worked out successfully. This sort of approach can prove useful not only in interacting with your children but also in other situations in your family life and work environment.

Sometimes when the emotions are too high or the moment is not right, the best option is to walk away—but before doing so, state that you need a moment to calm down. Do not be afraid to show vulnerability or transparency, as we all experience interactions that trigger high emotional responses.

We're all human. We lose our tempers, we get sad, we feel. The key here is to be aware of those emotions and then to take action or let go when we need to.

There are days when a lack of sleep or proper nutrition pushes me near the breaking point. Five or six situations will hit in rapid succession, and I'll be on the verge of going into meltdown mode. For example, I wake up later than I want, I spill coffee on my shirt while on my way to work, I forget a meeting, I suddenly remember that today is my baby's twelve-month check-up, my children leave messes all over the house, etc. These types of stressful moments happen weekly—if not daily—to all of us.

We can find ourselves responding negatively or with

knee-jerk reactions if we are not mentally and emotionally strong and well rested. But even in those difficult times, I am able to keep my cool when I work through these questions. And after everything settles, I'm able to talk about what's going on in a manner that is mindful and successful. I am not perfect, but I do forgive myself quickly and apologize for any bad decisions I may make. You are in control of recognizing your own feelings. You can tune in and be aware of your thoughts that will better guide your emotions. As you practice being mindful of your emotions and working through them, you will be able to check in with yourself when your emotions run high. All the tools you need are already sitting within you. You can guide yourself through hardships and life's challenges toward a more peaceful existence.

WORKBOOK

Chapter One Questions

Question: In what areas do you tend to view yourself as a victim of your life, as helpless, as overwhelmed, and as not in control? In what areas do you feel proactive, in charge, free, and able to make the best decisions?

_____

_____

_____

_____

_____

_____

_____

_____

_____

Question: What are some outward signs that you are allowing emotion to build up inside instead of dealing with it? You may call these coping mechanisms or survival techniques. How do different pent-up emotions change your responses toward others, especially those in your family?

_____

_____

_____

_____

_____

_____

_____

_____

_____

_____

_____

_____

Journal: Spend some time feeling and dealing—feeling each of your emotions without running from them and dealing with each one instead of blaming someone else for causing it. Why are you feeling what you are feeling? How will you accept each emotion? What action, if any, will you take?

Action: Set some emotional awareness breaks for yourself throughout the day. At each, ask yourself:

- What am I feeling right now?

- Why?

- What direct circumstances and indirect factors are contributing to my emotions?

- What physical symptoms of my emotions are present in my body?

- Is it time to act, to accept, or to fix?

Chapter One Notes

_____

_____

_____

_____

_____

_____

_____

_____

_____

_____

_____

_____

_____

_____

_____

_____

_____

_____

_____

_____

_____

CHAPTER TWO

Change Your Response

I was thirty-four years old. It was September 2016. I was six months into a new job that was unfamiliar and slightly disengaging compared to my previous position. I had come from a company where I'd worked for over twelve years and where I felt confident and capable. But at this new job, nothing was going right.

On top of this, my husband was significantly stressed with his own work, and our communication was broken. He was withdrawing, and I was stressed.

Then my nanny of almost four years decided it was time to move on with her life. She went back to school, and I was left to either find a new helper or do it all myself.

I was a mother of four children, ages 16, 10, 9, and 6. My eldest was in a troublesome relationship and hanging with a bad crowd. This child had begun demonstrating disrespect and making bad decisions, and was failing school. Meanwhile, I felt there was little I could do to help.

I remember going to the doctor with the weight of the world on my shoulders. I was not the woman I knew I could be. After only fifteen minutes of talking to me and not fully knowing me or my history, the doctor wrote me a prescription. This was a very surprising experience; I had just wanted to check my blood work and seek advice. It was this one experience that led me to become the advocate I am today for my health and my children's health.

After the visit to the doctor, I was determined and empowered to understand my mental state as well as my overall well-being. I became tuned into the importance of all areas of my life— emotional, physical, and mental. I decided that day to take back my mental and physical health.

I had already been an avid user of essential oils. Their powerful constituents had helped to heal my adult acne, but I now decided to tune into the implications of their organic chemical constituents for my mental stability. I began to develop healthy habits that incorporated the usage of essential oils, and I developed a holistic mindset to take back control of my health and my life.

My struggling child and I began to work through what was going on in their life, and I started to feel more clearheaded. I sought professional help from a therapist. My child and I met the therapist together and utilized the therapy sessions to work with each other. The therapy sessions provided an atmosphere where my child and I could share our concerns and disagreements without judging or interrupting each other. It was a significant help to our relationship.

Therapy has been instrumental in my relationship with my husband as well. We went through three different therapy sessions within our relationship, which also provided us with a safe environment to work through issues and learn to listen to each other. I highly recommend finding third-party professional help to work through all relationship problems, either alone or with the other person. Therapy helps focus the issues and provides the venue and the tools to work through them one by one, breaking down emotional barriers that sometimes clog or blur the issue. Therapy has been a relationship lifesaver for my marriage as well as my relationship with my kids, and it has made me a better wife, mother, and friend. It is important that you ask for help before you start to hold contempt within a relationship, as those feelings are hard, if impossible, to fix.

In January 2017, I made great strides in reducing my environmental toxins. My research on the impact that hormones from birth control have on our mental state startled me, so I adjusted accordingly. I also began to supplement daily with vitamins, and as mentioned above, I had started a consistent approach to utilizing essential oils in all aspects of my life. I wanted my mind and body to be as clear as possible. I was taking control of my life back.

Then things continued to change.

In February 2017, Children and Youth Services asked if my husband and I would take in a three-year-old boy who needed a home. The child was left with nowhere to go, so we welcomed him with open arms. Even though I felt my world was still out of control, I knew we were his best option.

It was now six months past the lowest point in my life—six months since the doctor appointment that helped me get my mind back in the game. But all of my problems were still there, and new difficulties seemed to be added daily. But I pressed on. Then on top of taking in our now adopted son, I got pregnant in April of 2017. After not having had a menstrual cycle for seven years, I seemed to have forgotten what those were for. All joking aside, this pregnancy only added to the pressure I was under.

How was I going to do this? How was I going to keep my flailing marriage together while fostering a little boy, raising my own four kids, taking on more responsibilities at work, dealing with chronic stress, and giving birth to a new baby?

That's when I had another moment of clarity. I found my way to the big picture and thought, "*I can do this and do it well!*" I took a deep breath, or more like several deep breaths, and made myself the number one priority. I revamped my approach, my life, my actions. Since that moment, I've been full of zest and drive to live out my dreams. I have been dreaming big. My big dreams may be little things, but I believe the baby steps are what make the big dreams.

I have taken the building blocks and foundations I was raised on and started to be more intentional with my team. I became more aware of my actions and the impact I had on others. I began owning my environment.

Over the past few years, I've revamped my mornings, made lists, taken practical steps toward my goals, meditated, eaten healthier, taken vitamins, worked on communication, read more, turned off the news, and tuned out the stuff I can't control.

I have never felt better. Because of the changes I've made, I'm free to love my life. I'm able to let go of what I can't control and change what I can. I changed how I responded to my life, and that has changed everything. Now I embrace each day with a smile and a hopeful bounce.

You Can Change

With any situation in life, we have two options. We can accept whatever is going on around us, or we can change it through modifying our actions and attitudes.

Once you've identified what's causing you to react, it's time to ask yourself a simple question: "What in this situation do I have the power to control and change?" This question is vital because you can only control your own actions. How you respond in a situation can cause a domino effect for yourself and for others. Not being mindful of your actions and your words can cause more negativity and spiral the situation out of control.

Think of the relationships you are involved in on a day-to-day basis. Perhaps it's with a close friend, your husband, or a child. If you are at work and you are presented with bad news, a common first reaction is to cast blame or deflect to someone else. However, passing blame or deflecting the issue never brings any good. It's better to be aware of your emotions first. Then, make the conscious decision to react in the best way possible to pursue your desired outcome.

You are the only person in control of yourself in any situation. You have the opportunity to change your response to whatever situation you find yourself in. Keep in mind that you can only control your own actions and attitudes in a situation—you can't change anyone else involved in a scenario. You have to determine what aspects of a circumstance you can and can't change, and act accordingly.

Because we are only in control of ourselves, there are external things we can't change. I had to learn this with my children. For about ten years, my husband and I struggled with raising strong-willed children. The more we tried to control them, the more we tried to protect them, the more they spiraled. Finally, we realized we couldn't change the child, but we could advise them and speak about our own experiences with the hope that they would pick up a few nuggets of wisdom along the way.

I had to come to the realization that I can't change my children or control their choices. I can control my focus on self-care while I do my best at being a good mother and wife. Here is the takeaway—I haven't changed any of my children. I can't change them. But I can and have changed the way I respond to their needs. I can guide them differently. I can parent them differently according to their individual needs. In the end, I can only be supportive of their decisions because they are individuals with their own ideas, thoughts, and desires.

As a mother of six, I find it fascinating how different each child is. They each have their temperament, personality, interests, desires, and dreams. As their mother, I know it is vitally important to view my children as unique individuals. I cannot parent or attend to each one of them the same. I need to be present and observe them, so that I can be the support that they need.

You cannot parent each child the same. They need to be approached, empowered, or championed differently. My children are very different, with vastly unique needs.

One child has always been strong-willed and spirited, ready to take on the world but having no desire to talk to or engage community or family members. She never required a large group of friends, nor appreciated or engaged in school dynamics.

Another child is a strong-willed, emotional child who has a tender heart but is also introverted and would rather play video games to be social than engage in in-person social groups. He excels at school with little to no effort.

The next child is easygoing and is always willing to engage and help around the house. He is a risk-taker and loves to be social and engage in peer groups, especially organized sports. He loves to be outside and is an excellent student who consistently works hard.

Another child is a free-spirited, emotional child who loves to be independent but also has a great knack at making friends. She is an artist at heart and sees school as social time. She is less focused on academics; however, she does very well when she applies herself and makes the time or is forced to make time.

The next child is a bright-eyed, spirited child that needs the love and attention all children deserve. He is highly intelligent and loves life. He is tuned into the family dynamics and loves to discuss the past. He is a hard worker and loves school.

My youngest differs greatly from the older kids in his temperament and abilities, and especially in his sleep habits. I look forward to observing and being mindful of him as he grows up as the youngest of six.

I mention each one of my children to show that they all have some similarities, as well as differences. This fact makes my job as mother unique and full of variables that are neither consistent nor controllable. Therefore, I only have control of how I respond to them.

It may be frustrating to realize you can't change a person or situation you're struggling with. It's in our human nature to want to change things, and it can be devastating when we can't. However, we can make an effort to work on our own reactions. That is the real change.

Working through our reaction to things we can't change is like practicing meditation. From the time I wake up till the time I go to bed, my mind is constantly racing with a thousand things to do, and there are times I become overwhelmed.

If I find myself in a negative thought spiral, such as thinking I am not good enough, and I feel pressure in my head, I stop and refocus. I do what is called my brain dump. I list everything, from what I'm worrying about to what I need to do. Then I organize everything on a piece of paper.

Only you have control of how you respond to a circumstance; only you are your true self-advocate. Be confident and believe that you can handle whatever happens. This approach really allows you to handle circumstances one day at a time. While you can't change people or every situation, you can always change how you respond and deal with them. You can change you.

Strategy for Change

To learn how to change your response to everything happening around you, you need a personal strategy. You will be amazed at how much it will help you in your everyday life. While each person's strategy looks a bit different, I'll share mine with you as a starting point.

First, I always have a notebook with me. In this notebook, I list everything I am worried about—my brain dump. Then I look at the information and prioritize what can be done quickly and what will require more time. I pause and gather any additional information I need; then I organize my thoughts and take action on the things I can take action on.

If you are a visual learner, like I am, writing down your concerns helps you see them as concrete and approachable.

I did this process with my husband, though at first, he was very resistant. I wanted to help him solve his problems, but that caused him to shut down and not even share his problems. I continued studying him and changing my approach until I found one that worked. Most importantly, I listened to him with empathy, rather than trying to "fix" him.

My husband eventually became open to the idea and

now asks me to do this brain-dumping process together with him. He says it helps him because he realized that even if he can't do XYZ today, he can visualize what *is* possible, which allows him to move forward with his next steps.

Second, I engage in meditation. I'm able to process my thoughts in as little as one minute; if I can get ten minutes, I'm able to accomplish so much more. Meditation doesn't have to be time consuming, but it will make the rest of your day more effective.

Third, I have taken ownership of my health, my self-love, and my routine. By changing the way I care for myself, I can respond gratefully to the life I've been given. On a daily basis, I do the following:

- Drink 16 ounces of water in the morning.

- Meditate each morning.

- Drink a bullet coffee, which consists of coffee, medium chain triglyceride oil (MCT oil), and various essential oils.

- Drink green juice/smoothie and prepare smoothie ingredients on Sundays for the week.

- Eat only healthy snacks, such as nuts and apples.

- Drink a minimum of 64 ounces of water a day.

- Incorporate yoga flow, rowing, and walks throughout the week to move my body.

- Dry brush, oil pull, and apply non-toxic chemical free oils and blends on my skin.

- Take a daily regimen of supplements and vitamins.

- Eat dinner at the family dinner table as much as possible, typically four or five times per week. I set a table each time we enjoy food as a family

- Attempt to get seven to eight hours of sleep (though babies certainly impede this!).

In addition to my daily routine, I also have a list of things I pursue monthly, bi-monthly, and bi-yearly. These changes in my routine have helped me stay grounded. By pursuing them, I have changed the narrative about my life. And because of that, I can gladly accept and manage the emotions and struggles that come up unexpectedly. Accomplishing these acts makes me feel empowered and in control.

- Schedule bi-monthly massages.

- Schedule hair and nail appointments months out and commit to them.

- Read on average two books per month, primarily fiction. I have replaced television with podcasts and books.

- Take time each week to review all of my calendars, plan my days, identify my gaps, ask for help where needed, keep a to-do list of all items, and prioritize them all into buckets.

- Review my buckets every month to ensure I am on track with where I want to be in the next month, year, and decade. I take these big-picture goals very seriously.

- Strive for a comfortable and clean home environment.

- Plan day trips for my family. My mother was amazing at this, taking my two brothers and me all over the place for fun getaways. She made things magical, and I strive to do the same for my family.

Prioritize What Matters

We waste a lot of energy trying to control things that are out of our power. This affects our physical health and wellbeing. If we aren't in good mental health, it's hard to stay physically healthy; our energy levels are low, and we can't seem to get good sleep.

With many of the world's problems, it's hard to process all that is going on around us. I think we want to solve problems when we hear about them, but we end up spreading ourselves too thin. We can't do everything well, and, when we try, we lose focus.

It's at this point that we need to decide what we really want out of life.

For me, I want to be present, aware, and connected with my children and my husband. I want to be fulfilled with the work I do. I want to invest time with my parents. I am protective of my time because I know how easily it can be wasted trying to change people, situations, and problems. We can't control it all, but we can focus on what's important. So what do you want out of life? What's important to you?

Finding your true goals will help you focus your energy. Too many individuals do not know what their true goals are, where they want to go, or what they want to be. They don't wake up telling themselves of their own self-worth. But all of this can be overcome. This is something you can change!

That is why it is so important to maintain self-care. You can take care of yourself and position yourself in a way that allows you to handle what comes up in your life financially, physically, or mentally. You can structure your life to meet your needs, or you can ask for help. This will allow you to adjust to those things that come your way and will help you compartmentalize, prioritize, and take action.

Changing how you respond to life empowers you to take action. You're ready to change the things that are in your power to change, you're ready to step up and take responsibility for your life, and you're willing to release the moments and situations that are outside of your control.

This is a place of peace. It is a place of growth. And you will discover you are much more capable than you ever thought.

WORKBOOK

Chapter Two Questions

Question: What are some things outside of your control that you spend emotional energy worrying about or trying unsuccessfully to change? How does this stress affect you? What could you change about your own response to each of these situations?

_____

_____

_____

_____

_____

_____

_____

_____

_____

_____

_____

Question: What do you want out of life? What is important to you? What are your top three to five life goals?

_____

_____

_____

_____

_____

_____

_____

_____

_____

_____

_____

Journal: Look at each important relationship and component of your life. Make a list of the things outside your control that you need to release or change your response to. Then list the positive changes that you are able to make that will improve your life and give you the ability to better accept the things you cannot change.

Action: Examine your morning routine. What are some simple changes you can make to be more focused and positive as you start each new day? Once you implement these, examine your daily routine, your weekly routine, your monthly routine, and your yearly routine. In each, look for changes that will help you care for yourself and enable you to release the things you cannot change.

Chapter Two Notes

_____

_____

_____

_____

_____

_____

_____

_____

_____

_____

_____

_____

_____

_____

_____

_____

_____

_____

_____

_____

CHAPTER THREE

Active Listening

I'm quick to give advice. It comes naturally to me to take action and control. I let my desires be known and am not afraid to say what I'm thinking or tell someone how things should be done. I tend to be a fixer and like to give advice. If my husband comes home from a bad day at work, I want to tell him how to fix his bad day. I tell my children how they should approach their homework or how to take a test better.

For many years, I was the one talking. But now I'm the one listening. Active listening is when one concentrates on what is being said, rather than just passively hearing the speaker.

I used to think listening meant breaking down the person's message and trying to relate to what was said. I thought being with someone meant talking to them and helping them fix their problems. Then I discovered the importance of simply being with someone and letting them talk without any strings attached. I found that if I'm not listening, I'm not growing as a person.

How to Listen Actively

Active listening feels unnatural because we are almost trained to talk about ourselves instead of being open to advice or hearing from others.

After having worked on my own listening skills, I found it very easy to find my people—the ones who hear me, want to listen to what I say, and love me for me. I also found there are people who do not listen or are unable to show up for me, and that is okay. The clarity allowed me to let go of hurt feelings of neglect and disrespect and to just love.

Once I understood active listening is something you have to work on, I realized that people who do not listen well are not mean or hateful, but unaware.

To effectively work through problems between people, it takes dedicated, active listening, as well as patience. There may be some people who are not ready to make whatever changes need to be made; and there may be those who are simply happy in their problems or situations. Whatever the case may be, solutions do not happen overnight. We cannot expect to see results in one week; rather, we will see small steps toward big changes.

If it seems like things turn silent, then that is a great time to begin the conversation and talk about what might be the issue or what might need to be worked through. Some people may not be ready to listen and may just want to talk. So listen to their stories, their frustrations, their problems—you'll never know how much that will mean to them. To this day, I am reminded of how my dad took the time to really listen to me when I was sorting through a problem.

When you are open and aware, you will find that people are more willing to open up and talk and share. They aren't necessarily open to hearing what you have to say, but they just want to be heard because they may feel as if they have no one to hear them.

Fully Engaging in Conversations

If you enter into a conversation having already decided that your views are correct, you aren't open or aware. You are having a conversation with yourself.

If you truly listen to what the other person says—even if your viewpoints are completely different or your upbringing is completely different—you will learn and grow. Your viewpoint will broaden. By actively listening and not making judgments on that person, you may hear them say something that is very inspiring, or they may take you down a path that you have never been on. They could show you a new approach or thought process that could help you.

This is something I've noticed in my relationship with my husband. I fell in love with him, married him, and chose to have a bunch of kids. There was, and is, a unique connection between us. We are polar opposites in regard to how we communicate, how we were raised, and how we approach problems. Rather than me assuming that he must change to be like me, I had to step back and realize

I only had control over changing myself. So, I started listening.

At first, I remember reacting strongly to the littlest offenses. He would say something, and I would be all over him with corrections, telling him how he should feel or react. It caused me to question our entire relationship at times! How can I be with someone who is so different from me? How will we make it?

Finally, I decided to just listen. I decided to do this every time we made the one-hour trek to visit his family. I'd sit there, not saying a word yet inwardly hating the silence. But then he started talking. He said very insightful things. Surprising things. I learned more about him—wonderful things!

I did this for five or six years; it didn't happen overnight. And I realized how much I'd let my own opinions dictate the way I thought he should have been when, in reality, he didn't need my help.

Then I started wondering if I needed to do the same with other people in my life. I started listening to everyone, people I liked as well as people I struggled with. And you know what? It's changing the way I see people in a good way.

Active listening is important on a professional level as well, as I noticed when I was a power system studies engineer/consultant. Somewhere along the line, I realized my job was to listen and to learn. My entire team, in fact, was comprised of good listeners. Aside from our technical acumen, we all practiced actively listening to find out what our customers wanted and then to provide them with the answers they needed, which played a big role in our success.

We helped answer questions and we were genuine, open, and transparent, which provided a great opportunity to develop strong work relations with all customers, peers, superiors, and individual contributors. Being an active listener allowed me to excel in my professional career and eventually carried over to my home as well.

Tips for Active Listening

Taking time to actively listen to others helps you identify the needs of others. It will also help you learn. You will find people will feel affirmed when talking with you, and they will want to keep talking!

Keep these tips in mind to be the best listener:

- Be aware and mindful of each situation you are in. This is not a natural practice, but it does affirm others who simply want to be heard.

- Be in a position where you put yourself in the other person's shoes, so you can empathize with them.

- Be willing to *not* be the center of attention, to allow the other person to know you are completely there for them. Silence is golden.

It's true. Active listening takes practice and a lot of work. As you develop the skill of meditation, your brain will begin to develop what it needs to listen well. You'll also be able to make others more comfortable as you create that natural, conversational listening atmosphere.

Active Listening at Home

Above, I explained how I learned to practice active listening in my relationship with my husband. Active listening is equally important and beneficial for other relationships within the home, such as those between siblings or between parents and children.

For instance, sometimes our teenaged children make unwise dating decisions, and it's our job as parents to work with them through these issues by truly listening to them. If we let them communicate their feelings, then we will be able to understand them better, and perhaps they will be better inclined to choose wise dating relationships.

As parents, we want to treat our teenaged children as adults, but when they get into trouble or get caught engaging in an unhealthy behavior, they have pushed the limit too far. When this happens—especially when they get caught doing the same thing repeatedly—I believe it is the child looking for attention. They want to be noticed. They want a reaction.

This can be a difficult position to be in as parents. It's even challenging on an emotional level, and it can be confusing when they are in turbulent stages. Still, we must practice active listening. Even when we're frustrated, hurt, or angry, we need to pause and let the kids share. We must let them tell us why they're doing what they're doing. We need to see it from their perspective.

Sometimes they surprise us and share more than we expect—perhaps even more than we think we want to know! However strange this may be, I think it's a good thing, as we are able to present advice to them. They may roll their eyes at us or tell us we are strict. Then we wonder, why do they want to share with us? Perhaps because they need to share with someone, and they may not have anyone else who will listen. As parents, we have a great responsibility and opportunity to simply listen to our teenaged children when they open up and share with us.

Parents should listen without strings attached. When teenagers are moving through adolescence, they naturally flock toward their peers and pull away from their parents. This creates an unconscious confusion since teenagers want to still be dependent on their parents, but they are naturally drawn to their peers. As parents, we must be patient and learn to listen before taking action.

Our children need to feel as if they can manage and take action on their lives, so the balance is difficult. It comes down to creating a loving, stable environment where the child feels worthy of love and connection. Then, when a parent does have to lay down a strong line of control with the child, the foundation is set for the parent to stand on and the child understands the parent is on his or her side.

We may be afraid we will push our children away while they are in this growing stage of life, but it actually provides the chance to bring them closer to us. We have the opportunity to create a safe place for them as they explore their thoughts and feelings and decide what they want to do in life.

For instance, one of my children, who has a full-time job as a hairstyle assistant, works really hard and is learning how to navigate the working relationship with their boss. I have really learned to listen, thus creating a safe environment where they are comfortable talking to me about what they are dealing with in their personal life, relationships, and job. No matter how old we are, we always need someone who will be there just to listen.

Active Listening at Work

Being in the corporate environment, I find I have gotten a lot of input, feedback, direction, and mentorship simply by being a good listener. That means sitting across the table and asking questions and truly listening to the answers. I'm not just asking questions so I can be heard or so I can sound like I know what I'm talking about. I am asking questions so that my superiors and subordinates feel heard, and surprisingly, it also develops trust. It develops a bridge that helps me stay positive.

Listening helps me to write better scopes and develop projects more fully. It helps me give direction and make personal connections. It helps me support my team because, by listening to them, I can better understand them. I can anticipate their needs and frustrations. I can provide them with what they need to succeed.

Listening also helps my work companions to be there for me when I need it. If I've been attentive to them in the past—if I've listened to them and heeded their advice and warnings—they're also going to come to my aid when I need them most.

Much of a career is about the relationships you make. You want relationships with those above you and those below you. You even want relationships with those in different departments. You never know who is going to help you or get you through a roadblock.

When I was hired as a twenty-two-year-old in my job as an electrical engineer, I was told on the first day that they had hired me as a professional and would treat me as a professional. My boss, along with his entire team, was a wonderful mentor and his confidence in me helped me flourish.

He trusted me to figure things out on my own and to conduct research when I did not know answers. He encouraged me to never be fearful that I was going to be wrong or that I was going to be judged. This gave me the confidence to have no fear of making mistakes. The excellent mentorship from my boss and his team provided me with a great foundation for my career, and I try to create that same environment for others.

Investing in Relationships

Everyone is on a different path, with different experiences and different cultures. If we can learn to be open-minded, loving, and compassionate, we will be able to discover things about ourselves and learn from others. By engaging in listening, we can be in tune with others' facial expressions, body movements, and comfort levels. We can then cater to what puts them at ease, creating an inviting experience where people will feel comfortable opening up.

I'll never forget when one of my peers thanked me for asking what she thought about an issue. It really surprised me because the gratitude was genuine. In my world I ask about people's thoughts all the time, but it must have been a rare gesture in her world. By asking for her input, I created an atmosphere in which she felt empowered. I made a way for her to share.

Sometimes it takes huge effort on my part to keep from just saying what I think. But the more I practice active listening, the more I realize that others just want to be heard.

If you're one to continually give advice or speak up whenever there's a lull in the conversation, consider stepping back and evaluating the situation before deciding to jump in. Just because you're saying something, doesn't mean you're handling the situation correctly. Take the time to intentionally listen to others, and you'll be surprised at the outcome.

WORKBOOK

Chapter Three Questions

Question: Are you more of a talker or a listener? Describe someone in your life who has given you the gift of truly listening to you. How did it feel to have someone allow you to share without judging or inserting himself or herself? When have you done this for someone else?

_____

_____

_____

_____

_____

_____

_____

_____

_____

_____

_____

Question: Who are some people with whom you are frequently annoyed or whose perspective on life drives you crazy? How can you intentionally begin actively listening to them with an open-minded, empathetic attitude?

_____

_____

_____

_____

_____

_____

_____

_____

_____

_____

Journal: As you start listening, you will learn so much about others—and even about yourself. What are some things you have learned about the people closest to you? As you listen across weeks and months, what trends do you see about what is important to them, about their strengths and weaknesses, about their hurts, hopes, and vulnerabilities? Begin creating a character sketch of each of your family members based on what you have learned from listening to them.

Action: Prepare some simple, open-ended questions that you can use with your spouse/partner, children, coworkers, and friends. Plan a time in the next week where you will be present and listen to them without your own agenda. Keep in mind that for some relationships and situations, silence may be better than asking questions.

Chapter Three Notes

CHAPTER FOUR

Slowing Down

In a world where parents are busy taking children to their extracurricular activities, it's interesting to see how disengaged the relationships seem. Gone are the days of family time. Everyone is busy running from here to there and not making time to slow down and enjoy precious moments. I've experienced it with my own children. If we aren't intentional about family time, we can quickly become detached from one another. When other parents share how chaotic their schedules are, it makes me feel stressed. I don't want that for my life. So when my kids started playing soccer and other sports, I knew I needed a plan—and my plan seems to have worked.

I find that I'm very relaxed when showing up to the occasional soccer game, even though I have my own intense career schedule and family schedule. And everyone always asks, "How do you do it?" My response? "One sport and one season." I only allow each of my children to be involved in one activity per season—otherwise, we all end up spread too thin.

Having structure and taking it one step at a time is the trick to slowing down. I truly believe the time to just be present at home is monumental. The slow days, the creative days, the nature walks, the picnics, and the no-plan days are a great example of everyday life as you get older. It is vital to learn being content with the mundane so we can tune into the magical moments of just being.

The Importance of Structure

Children thrive on structure; therefore it is best to let them choose one activity to be involved in for the season. This will prevent you, and them, from being pulled around and caught up in the chaos. There is a sense, though, that kids need to be in multiple things and that we are keeping them from experiencing life when we limit their involvement. But it's okay if your kids miss out! They need to learn how to prioritize their interests.

The truth is, you can create a low-stress oasis around yourself and your family by slowing down and being selective in terms of activities. Anything else will be chaos. With my children, I ask them if they want to play sports, and they pick one. If they get disengaged halfway through the year and want to quit, they must finish out the season. They do have the opportunity to readjust at the next sign-up. Soon, they know what they want to do and why they want to do it. This gives them drive and purpose. It helps them zero in on their passions.

It's also important as a family to determine what things

are important. Just as your individual children can be running from activity to activity, families can also get caught up in a desire to do it all. Prioritizing and scheduling family time is how you make the most of your down time.

Slowing Down as a Family

Life and time are precious, so it's important to take a step back and slow down as a family. You can't enjoy each other if you are overfilling your schedules, pushing and pulling people in different directions.

The only way to accomplish family time is by establishing a structured routine for yourself. I am very aware of what I want to accomplish in a day, week, or month. One of my goals is to have quality time with my kids, such as being able to go jump on the trampoline on a whim or walk through the park.

My family almost always has dinner together—that's another one of my goals. If you have smaller children, you can make it a point to be a part of their nighttime routine. Spend the last few moments of their day talking about what they did and engaging in conversation with them.

By structuring your day for what works for the family, you'll be able to function at a high level. You'll be able to do the things that are important to everyone. Of course, you'll need to make adjustments along the way. You'll need to find how best to spend family time, but the key is to always make sure you are creating an environment that allows them to be who they are. In the long run, this will have a lasting impression because you took the time for them while they were young.

The Cost of Not Slowing Down

The effects of not slowing down are like choosing not to be mindful of the food you eat. In today's fast-paced society, everyone is looking for that quick meal—like a microwave dinner or a pre-mixed protein shake—on the way to the next event.

Simply reaching for the easiest thing means we end up eating food that is terrible for us. The more bad food we eat, the more likely we are to become obese, sick, and sluggish. When our health dips, our entire mindset dips with it. We lose confidence, become lazy, and adopt a passive lifestyle.

The same can be said of not taking time to slow down. Sure, it's easier to just stay busy. It's easier to fill our schedules, because being busy feels important and it keeps our minds off our issues. However, there is so much more benefit to being deliberate with our time, to slowing down for what's healthy instead of chasing after what's easy.

The Benefit of Slowing Down

Slowing down will allow you to be present with one another. You'll have the opportunity to connect on a deeper level. It will give you the opportunity to listen to what's going on in everyone's lives and talk about concerns or frustrations. I have found that my children have become much more open with me since I have taken the time to slow everyone down.

By slowing down, you will become more physically

active, too, with more time for healthy activities like taking walks, working in the yard, and going on bike rides. By being less busy, you'll do more of the stuff that matters. Your kids will connect with neighbor kids, they'll play in the yard, and you'll attend block parties. You'll get to know the family down the street. Your neighborhood will become your friends, your village.

Lastly, it's important to be with your kids consistently during a specific time of the day—often nighttime—to settle yourselves and reflect on the day's events. During this time, you can teach them to practice personal self-care and hygiene and why it's important to get a full night's sleep.

If parents or other caregivers are not able to be around for the evening hours, it may be wise to implement a different time where they can connect with their children about the children's days, weeks, and months. We should make sure we regularly check in with all those we are in important relationships with, such as our significant others, family, friends, and work colleagues.

Strategies for Slowing Down

To get started, try these strategies:

- Check your motives and reasons for why you want such a busy life. Is it worth it? Your schedule is what is preventing you from slowing down. Only you can make that change.

- Self-reflect and slow yourself down first. Then,

you can slow your family down.

- Practice self-care because when you start caring for yourself, you are in a much better place overall. I've found that if you are able to make this change for yourself, then your family will follow suit.

- Slow down your mind and organize your thoughts.

- Summarize your problem(s) using the whole meditative approach—which is quieting your mind and focusing only on that what needs your attention.

Another aspect of foundational health that goes hand in hand with slowing down is conflict prevention. Because I have so many kids, there is a lot of conflict resolution going on. I have learned to approach their tantrums and fights calmly, and because of that, they are always working together and working out their differences.

The Downside of Technology

We all need human connection, and technology can provide that to a small extent. But there is a downside to all that screen time. Devices create less engagement and less interaction within the family unit. Not having conversations means no one is dealing with their feelings or engaging in conflict resolution. More screen time means fewer opportunities to help others navigate through life.

We have rules to prevent this from happening in our family. There are to be no electronic devices at the table or at any family functions. If a car ride is less than an hour and a half, the electronic devices must be turned off. For the half hour before bedtime, my kids can either go outside or read books.

Having rules likes these creates boundaries for using technology, because when we create and establish boundaries and have conversations, then we're more willing to talk about important things. We begin to see how we are growing, and we also see the importance of engaging with one another.

Benefits of Disconnecting

Because we are so connected to our devices, we are not paying attention to relationships in our workplace and at home. We also aren't able to do our biggest thinking.

A large benefit of disconnecting from technology is that it forces you outside. You'll make more friends and explore more. It helps your kids do better in school—socially and academically.

If disconnecting your children from technology for a time is new territory for you, then, as it is with any change, you will need to take baby steps along this journey. But don't give up. Fight for every little bit. Your family may resist, but you can win them over.

Stop and Enjoy Life

Our culture values busy schedules and doing activities.

We sign our kids up for as much as they want, and then we wonder why we aren't connecting. Why don't we have family time? Why don't we talk?

The pull toward an events-driven lifestyle or a technology-driven lifestyle can easily seep in and drain family conversations and relationships. It's time to develop structural measures and effective strategies that work for you and your family in relation to slowing down and enjoying each other as a family unit. Doing so will help you manage your time and make the most of every moment. It's part of the journey toward a better you.

Let me give you some practical suggestions that will allow you to better manage technology:

- Cleanse your computer. Organize desktop folders and clean the hard drive regularly.

- Cleanse your inbox. Start an unsubscribe folder and take one day a month to unsubscribe from unwanted email.

- Set boundaries for your e-mail. Set new rules for yourself to check your inbox only twice per day.

- Cleanse your phone. Begin by deleting apps you don't use anymore. Organize apps into folders so that you only have one screen of apps. Turn off all notifications in the settings section.

- Cleanse your calendar. Take everything on your calendar and put it in a notebook. Circle the priorities that need to stay. Decide to automate, delegate, or eliminate everything else.

- Cleanse your social media. Unfollow friends and pages that no longer align with who you are becoming. Set new boundaries for how often you will check social media platforms.

WORKBOOK

Chapter Four Questions

Question: What routines, traditions, and relationship-builders are important for your family inside the home? Are these getting pushed aside because of overcommitment to outside activities?

_____

_____

_____

_____

_____

_____

_____

_____

_____

_____

Question: Is technology a friend or foe to your family? What guidelines can you set for each member of the family so that technology serves your goals rather than enslaves you?

_____

_____

_____

_____

_____

_____

_____

_____

_____

_____

_____

_____

Journal: What activities are vital for yourself and your family to be involved in, and which ones are filler? Make a list of all of your family's actives outside the home and then reorder the list by priority. Priority should be determined based on how well these activities are fulfilling long-term goals. Are you spending too much time on things that don't have much long-term reward?

Action: Write down the benefits to slowing down yourself and your family. Now write down your fears about making this sort of lifestyle change. Then choose one thing that you can immediately and rather effortlessly cut from your life and dream about how doing so can begin a process toward greater freedom and more family time.

Chapter Four Notes

CHAPTER FIVE

Managing Your Actions

There are lots of books out there about how to manage your time. It seems expert after expert has weighed in on this topic to varying degrees of success. But isn't it all a bit misleading? Time is not something to be managed. It can't be managed, because it can't be changed.

But we can manage our actions. And by doing this, we can make better use of our time.

Managing our actions means being in control. It's the idea of taking ownership, creating boundaries, and being disciplined with how you spend your time. It's tackling the day with your own to-do list. It's called being proactive.

Be Tuned In

So often, we focus our energy on putting out fires. We're reactive to things around us, which is why our time feels so outside of our control.

To manage your actions you need to be tuned in, aware, and mindful of how you approach your daily, weekly, or monthly tasks. This means being aware and disciplined enough to work on tasks that haven't yet made it to emergency status.

Truly, all of this takes practice and time. Because I had parents who grounded me in the strength of being mindful of my thoughts and emotions, I was able to adapt quickly to the busy schedules of high school and then college. I learned how to manage my time so that I could accomplish all I wanted to accomplish. By the time I took on a full-time job as a bartender, working forty hours while also going to school, I was confident in my actions and choices in life.

I worked forty hours and was also able to manage my school workload. I started tuning in and developing relationships with colleagues, while also being extremely focused on all of my tasks.

I became even more cognizant of time management after I met my husband.

I've always been one who takes on a lot. I had two jobs shortly after I met my husband. I worked Thursday to Sunday as a bartender and then full-time as an engineer in my new position. At twenty-two, when I committed to caring for his daughter on the weekend, I quit my part-time job at the bar.

My whole family thought I was crazy for taking on so many responsibilities at such a young age. But I did, and it worked. I had a lot on my plate, but I confidently took the actions needed to keep it all running smoothly. I began to realize that I was capable of far more than I had thought.

Many people use the excuse of not having enough time. It's the number one reason why people don't meet deadlines at work or respond to emails in a timely manner. It's also the primary reason why many don't pursue hobbies or dreams or relationships. They find themselves inadvertently saying, "I don't have time." Their assessment always ends up being correct. They don't think they have the time, and then they find out that they were right.

But what if it's that very mindset that is the problem?

Instead of using time as an excuse, set boundaries with the amount of time you have. What if you took control of your responses and your actions and found that you can make time for the things you love and the people you love?

The only catch is that you can't do it all, or at least you can't do it all alone.

Get Help

If you are cognizant of all that you want to do, you will eventually need help from others. Having a clear idea of how and when you need help is key to taking successful action steps. In other words, define the help you need and find a way to get it.

But don't assume you will get it for free or from family.

When we were just starting out in our marriage, my husband was a bartender and I was making a mediocre engineering salary. Times were tough. We were making it, but just barely. He worked the night shift and I worked the day shift, and it became very obvious that we needed help to aid us with the household and with childcare. I could have relied on my parents for childcare assistance, but I didn't. I knew that would be asking too much of them. We have built our family with the help of five lovely nannies. We hold each of them close to our hearts, and I know I could not have done it without them. Having help allowed me to pay attention to my children's emotional and spiritual needs when I came home from work.

For you, this may look very different. There are a number of ways we can employ others to make our lives more doable. The important thing here is to figure out your needs, goals, and expectations. Communicate with your spouse or your loved ones. Then, work from there.

Baby Steps

My team members at work are daily reminders of how some people excel at certain things while others struggle. Even the simple task of answering the phone is a great example. Some return phone messages quickly. Others may never even check their voicemail. Some are comfortable talking on the phone. Others show noticeable stress.

Everyone is different. But even if you are not good at managing your actions, you can always take baby steps to improve. It's like exercising. There are people who start with walking or jogging before they move to running. And there are those who simply prefer to walk or jog, which is perfectly fine too. Each person is different, and each person will handle things differently.

The important thing is that you do something to move forward, because the alternative is a life of missed goals, forgotten dreams, and constant chaos.

I have discovered that several things tend to happen if we don't manage our actions well:

- Our self-worth is lower, and therefore we have less energy.

- We are impatient with our spouse, short with our children, or annoyed with coworkers.

- We slip into a negative spiral.

But if we seek to manage our actions well, we create synergy with everyone we come into contact with; we see the fruit of improvement in our relationships with our family and others.

I am a fairly driven person and like to create and set goals for myself with milestones to achieve those goals. Over time, I can see and feel the progress I am making, and that keeps me going. When I feel like I am not making the kind of progress I want, I sense tension. That forces me to tune into myself so I can refocus. I usually ask myself why I am not making progress, and that helps me re-channel my attention and direction.

When we strive to manage our actions well, there is an aspect of self-care that's required, which is extremely important because you are not the only one affected by your actions. If you are not intentional with your actions and do not take the time to structure your days, weeks, and months, you end up being low on energy and frazzled.

However, if you put yourself first and tend to your mind, health, and soul, task management becomes second nature. Moreover, you learn to take on the items that bring you passion and outsource or ask for help regarding the areas that you don't excel in and that bring you less joy. Self-care allows you to follow your passions and provides the clarity and attention your life needs.

For instance, if you want to accomplish certain things with your family, you must make a point to set goals, make lists, and discuss what you need to accomplish. Failing to do so means the whole family will miss out on those accomplishments or activities together. Taking proper care of yourself, in turn, causes good energy in your home or workplace or wherever you are. It fuels your desire to succeed.

It may seem selfish to practice self-care, but the opposite is true. Self-care recharges you in such a way that it allows you to give back to others in a much bigger, more multiplied way. So thirty minutes for yourself may result in days of focused time and care for the people you love.

Managing Actions Well

Managing our actions can look daunting at the outset because it requires dedication and focus. But if given the right tools, managing our actions is rewarding and a great timesaver. Here are some tips and practices for managing your actions well:

Develop and have an action-management system that works for you. In that system, write down appointment times, bill payments, you-time—everything you need to accomplish in a day, a week, and a month goes into your system that helps keep you organized.

Put your action-management system where you can see it first thing every morning. Then, move through those things throughout the day as you accomplish each task. If you are going to be out and about and not near the main action-management system, use notes or something else as a reminder, especially if you can't get to a task you had planned for. You can also review your task list at certain times of the day or week to help you keep the system moving.

Break large tasks down into mini goals or steps. This is effective because many goals can't be done all at once.

Reset yourself each Sunday night. You can reset by looking over last week's goals, crossing items off the list, or moving tasks to the coming week's goals; then, you can make adjustments for whatever you need.

It's perfectly okay to admit that you struggle. After all, we all struggle with different things. If you struggle with managing your actions, here is some encouragement:

- If you find yourself in a rut, unable to do it all, give yourself permission to fail. Tell yourself you are perfect just as you are.

- If you find yourself unable to do things, tell yourself "I can." Invite someone to hold you accountable, and make a point to keep your list of goals in front of you.

- If you find yourself talking negatively, stop and

start over. Being positive is the most rewarding quality we can have for ourselves and for others.

Managing your actions to make the most efficient use of your time takes deliberate effort. But if you keep moving forward, accomplishing one or two baby steps at a time to make necessary changes, you will see growth.

WORKBOOK

Chapter Five Questions

Question: When have you used "I don't have enough time" as an excuse to avoid doing something you didn't want to do? What time-consuming hobby, project, or goal have you been able to accomplish in spite of a busy schedule because it was important to you? What does this say about the reality of action management?

_____

_____

Question: What are some ways you can hire or enlist help? Who are some people who would love to be part of your team? What are some unrealistic expectations you have placed on yourself? For what things can you get help so you can focus on higher priority items?

_____

_____

_____

_____

_____

_____

_____

_____

_____

_____

_____

Journal: What do you already do well in your action management? In what areas do you need to improve? Where are you in a rut? Where do you need accountability? Where do you need to replace negative self-talk with positive belief?

Action: Research different action/time management systems and try one that you think will work for you. Commit to using it fully for at least a month to decide if it is the right system for your personality and lifestyle. Be sure to do a daily review and a weekly reset.

Chapter Five Notes

CHAPTER SIX

Self-Care

It is customary to tell our friends and family that life is busy, but we're content. But then in those quiet moments of being alone, we are faced with the reality of things. Maybe we feel lost or forgotten. Maybe we struggle to remember our goals and dreams. Maybe we can't remember the last time we have enjoyed time to just *be*. All of these are signs that maybe we aren't caring for ourselves the way we should. Maybe our quest to meet everyone's need has made it so that our own needs have gone unmet.

Statistics show that many people are unhappy.[2] Maybe some of us feel sadness because we are worried about our health, lifestyle, family—whatever it may be. Maybe some of us are afraid to do things differently and take action. It's normal to feel stuck, but being stuck is not a feeling that needs to be with you forever.

If you feel drained, forgotten, or tired, then it's time for some self-care. Filling your body with goodness and positivity will allow you to get unstuck, engage, and be present in the work you do and with the people you love. What feels good to you? What restores your energy? What makes you feel empowered? The answers to these questions—whatever those answers may be—is the meaning of self-care. Though it may sound contradictory, those small decisions to do something good for yourself have a huge impact over time. By choosing self-care, you will see positive change, such as successful goal-setting and mental clarity.

This can be as simple as giving yourself ten minutes every day, or making a green drink, or meditating for a few moments. I do all of those things every morning, in addition to ten minutes of stretching, and the change I have seen is immeasurable. These small steps help me to feel my best.

But what does it mean to feel our best? We've forgotten. We're so accustomed to putting bad food in our bodies, to not getting enough sleep, and to accepting the negative thoughts we have about ourselves. We're so used to just existing and to being lethargic.

We think feeling our best means keeping up with the Joneses, buying the latest gadget, or getting a bigger house. However, these things will never feed our minds. They will never help us set and hit goals. They will never help us be our best inside and out.

Self-care—true self-care—is designed to focus on what's important. Practicing self-care means to cut through the unfulfilling way of life we have come to accept and embrace something better.

Self-Care Basics

There are several things I do to practice self-care. Keep in mind that what works for me may not be what works for you. Some of my practices may not even appeal to you, but I share my routine simply as a guide. Eventually the goal should be that you feel confident and comfortable enough to come up with your own self-care system.

- I tune into how I am feeling in the present moment and pay attention to my current demands. I ask, "What are those demands doing to me?"

- I write down what I'm grateful for each day.

- I ask myself questions like, "Where am I going?" "What has been asked of me?" "What do I want to have accomplished today, this week, this month?" Answering these questions helps me be more definitive in how I write down my goals.

- I list my three priorities for the day, allowing myself to see what I have accomplished and how long things take me.

- At the end of the day, I reflect on what I have accomplished during that day.

Practicing self-care means living out our core fundamental needs: to be active and productive and to have community. Self-care is an action in and of itself and it will foster within you a better way to love and serve those around you. Self-care attracts a community.

One of my self-care focuses has been getting into essential oils. After having much personal success with the products, I decided to host an essential oils class. Six people attended my class—a strong turnout for this type of thing.

I asked them, "What do you want to change?"

The women, ages 23 to 65, all said, "We want more energy." "We want to sleep better." "We want reduced pain." I was able to teach them a different approach for achieving all those things through oils and also share ideas on instilling daily healthy habits.

Because I have invested in myself and taken the time to learn essential oils, I am able to take what I have gained and spread it to others, making their lives better. Self-care allows you to give more to others.

Even more importantly, you are valuable and worth being cared for. No one is going to care for you better than yourself! If you do not practice self-care on a regular basis, you will miss the opportunity to show yourself grace.

You will miss the opportunity to be healthy and therefore live longer.

You will miss out on reduced stress and reduced inflammation.

You will miss out on a stronger immunity.

You will miss out on being fully present.

You will miss out on having time and energy for your precious family or other significant relationships in your life because you won't be ready to hit the ground running as soon as you wake up.

When I am not consistently practicing self-care, my

husband and I can be like two sailboats passing by one another at a distance, not connecting. But when I tune into my needs and care for myself, I'm much more aware of my natural tendency to go through life individually and I am able to make some intentional changes so that we can connect more.

Practicing Mindfulness

Let me give you some practical examples of practicing mindfulness. I begin each day with a ten-minute session of sitting still and being with my thoughts. I started with five minutes and have built my routine up to at least ten minutes. This allows me to set my mindset for the day. Our mindset is a collection of attitudes that determines how we will respond to challenges, how we will manage tasks for the day, and how we will care of ourselves.

I also start the day meditating on what I am grateful for and, more specifically, what I was grateful for the day before. Meditation can change one's life. It can strengthen the immune system, enhance sleep, and improve human connection.

Dr. Mark Hyman, a leading expert in functional medicine and holistic health, has stated, "Your thoughts have real and measurable effects on your body and brain. Your immune cells know your deepest feelings."[3] Your mind and body are always listening to your self-talk. Your thoughts are your beliefs.

I believe if everyone knew the power of a negative thought, they would never have another negative thought again. When I find myself entering a negative thought cycle, I am able to be mindful or envision the negative self-talk and picture the detriment it is doing to my cells to help me change my mindset.

When I eat now, I am very mindful of what the food is and how my body will use it for energy. I have changed my way of thinking to not be about weight gain or weight loss, but rather about cell strength and energy levels. I am therefore mindful of how food is either hurting me or healing me. Creating a healthy balance with food leads to a wonderful, easy approach to healthy eating.

Structuring and being intentional with my time is also an example of mindfulness. I make time to clean up my calendar daily, weekly, and monthly. I take time to check in regularly on my to-do lists—home, work, financial, kids, husband, family—and track that I am spending my time where I want to invest my energy.

I develop goals and identify growth opportunities. I am goal conscious by focusing on my destination, motivating myself, and regularly challenging myself. However, I am also growth conscious in the sense that I focus on my journey. I enjoy maturing and growing those around me. I know it is not the destination but the journey that matters, and therefore, I continue to grow past the goals I set.

As I approach each day, I am mindful of the fundamentals for growth: I continually challenge myself. My focus is always forward. I surround myself with an affirming atmosphere. I am excited to wake up each day. I do no fear failure.

Don't Give In to Guilt

You can't pour from an empty cup. By the end of the day, if you feel so exhausted that you cannot give anything more, then you need to do what makes you happy until you are ready to be present for those who need you.

We can feel guilty at times, however. If we need extra "me" time to recharge, we think we're being selfish—yet in that we've got it all wrong. You aren't giving your family your best when you're unhappy and unfulfilled.

Perhaps you think you shouldn't care for yourself because you don't really know what will make you happy. Perhaps you're afraid to be alone with your thoughts. You're afraid to take that time for yourself because what if it doesn't help your mindset? Or perhaps you're afraid of what you'll discover. You're afraid that some time for reflection will reveal how bad your marriage really is. Or it will prove that you do indeed need to switch careers.

Being alone with your thoughts has the potential to bring up a lot of things that may or may not be desirable. But in no way should we allow this to rule over us. We shouldn't feel guilty for doing the right thing and taking care of ourselves.

Self-Care Activities

Self-care doesn't need to be an expensive manicure or an hour alone. It can be simple and meaningful without taking up a lot of time or money. Here are some ways you can enjoy self-care:

- Be wise with your eating habits. We are all aware that we get our energy from what we eat, so be aware of what you feed your body and pay attention to the nutrients and food you indulge in.

- Be aware of what type of people you surround yourself with. If you see the need, create boundaries for toxic people in your life. Realize who they are and how they make you feel.

- Be aware of what you want. These are the areas of life that are most important to you—the areas that you may find yourself thinking about the most, such as: body and wellness, emotional and spiritual health, relationships, parenting, work, money and finances, or community and giving.

- Move your body. Keep your body mobile and engage in some kind of movement throughout the day. Focus on feeling great, not on losing weight.

- Rest. Be cognizant of your sleep habits and protect that time. Studies say you need seven to nine hours of sleep a night. Tune into that.

- Take time for yourself to reflect on your days and weeks.

Because our thoughts and feelings create action, we must be aware and mindful of what those thoughts are and how they are affecting others by our actions. If we take action with the things that help us live successful lives, we will be able to experience life to the fullest.

WORKBOOK

Chapter Six Questions

Question: When do you most often tend to feel drained, forgotten, or tired? What routines do you have in place for self-care, and what most often leads to neglecting those routines?

_____

_____

_____

_____

_____

_____

_____

_____

_____

_____

Question: How can self-care enable you to more effectively care for your loved ones? In what ways do you battle guilt or fear regarding choosing self-care? How might self-care look different in different seasons of your life?

_____

_____

_____

_____

_____

_____

_____

_____

_____

_____

_____

_____

Journal: Make a list of the activities and actions that restore your energy. How long does each one take? Is there a cost involved? How and when can you work these activities into your self-care routine?

Action: Plan at least an hour this week to spend time alone and create a plan for regular, energizing self-care. Look at the changes you need to make to your time, your diet, your community, and your attitude. How will you begin to incorporate these changes through establishing habits of self-care?

Chapter Six Notes

CHAPTER SEVEN

Holistic Health

Holistic health focuses on functional medicine that takes a self-advocacy approach to health and self-care, aiming at understanding the whole self. The idea is that by being healthy on all three levels—physical, emotional, and spiritual—you are able to have clarity on where you are in your life to prevent, or even possibly eradicate, disease.

The message is loud and clear, especially with the breakdown of our health-care system—we are living shorter and dying longer. In fact, our health-care system should be renamed disease-care system. We must develop healthy eating and living habits in order to get the most out of our lives.

I would like to summarize some healthy habits that I have implemented in my life over the years that align with the approach of holistic health:

- Eliminate environmental toxins by cleansing and detoxifying your environment. We are bombarded with environmental toxins— household air is times more toxic than outside air. Eliminate fragrances and chemicals within your cleaning and body products and start to utilize non-chemical, environmentally friendly products instead.

- Rest and manage stress by calming your mind and grounding your intentions. You should also prioritize a healthy sleep environment. Sleep improves mood and gives your body the time to repair and regenerate.

- Exercise and move for physical health and to soothe the mind. Regular exercise strengthens the muscles and supports the cardiovascular, circulatory, and lymphatic systems.

- Eat right to ensure you are fueling, supporting, and fortifying your mind, body, and soul. A healthy, thriving body starts with daily nutrition and digestive support. Did you know that your gut contains so many neurons, it's essentially your second brain?

All of these healthy habits involve lifestyle changes that promote self-care and proactive medical care. Ultimately, they are all versions of true health care—protect and restore.

The list of habits I've included here has been helpful in my pursuit of a healthy, balanced life. I hope you'll use and expand upon these tips for yourself. Start with baby steps—incorporate a few at a time:

Environmental Detox

- Surrounded yourself with plants. They are not only good for the air you breathe in your home, but also for your mental state.

- Install Himalayan salt lamps in each room to help purify the air and eliminate free radicals.

- Unplug for at least two waking hours every day and for one full day each week—check out to check in.

- Limit the amount of screen time (TV, iPhone, etc.) after sundown and wear blue light blocking glasses when you do use electronics for long periods of time.

- Put your phone in airplane mode while you sleep.

- Stop watching the news or reading the paper incessantly. Use that time to listen to or read something that will develop you as a person to create the change you want to see in the world.

- Remove all Teflon™ pans and plastics from your kitchen and replace them with ceramic, cast iron, glass, and stainless steel to ensure happier hormones

- Use only all-natural, aluminum- and paraben-free deodorant. Note—the transition takes patience to allow your system to detox, so beware!

- Eliminate any products that have the ingredient triclosan. Top offenders are hand soap and toothpaste.

- Spend time in nature as much as possible.

- Strive to do something daily that causes your body to sweat.

- Develop a minimalist mindset.

- Whittle down the number of products you use daily on your skin and in your home.

- Remove all air fresheners from your home and place an essential oil diffuser in each room instead.

- Install a filter or water treatment system to remove toxins from your water supply.

Physical Health

- Implement a weekly meal preparation day every week to ensure convenient, healthy meals each week.

- Drink 16 ounces of water first thing each morning.

- Drink water between meals, consuming at least half your body weight in ounces of water every day. For an extra bonus, add a drop of lemon, grapefruit, or lime essential oil to each glass.

- Make greens the center of your meals and even add them to your morning smoothies. Greens are rich in vitamins, minerals, omega-3, and folate.

- Take an excellent, quality probiotic every day for gut biome, brain, and immune system, as well as a bioavailable multivitamin, omega-3 supplement and digestive enzyme.

- Remove as much dairy and gluten as possible from your diet.

- Do not eat after 8 p.m.

- Eliminate refined sugar from your diet. Read labels - sugar is everywhere. You can indulge your sweet tooth with low-glycemic-index fruits, such as blackberries, blueberries strawberries, and a little 80 percent dark chocolate.

- Find creative ways to consume healthy fats on a daily basis from foods such as nuts, avocados, coconut, and fish oils.

- Apply a simple body oil of fractionated coconut oil and two or three drops of essential oil to damp skin after a shower.

- Schedule a massage twice a month.

- Dry brush your skin before every shower.

- Purchase a trampoline for your backyard to play with your kids and promote healthy lymph flow.

- Take an Epsom salt bath at least once a week.

- Get to bed before 10 p.m.

Emotional Health

- Schedule a weekly date with your spouse.

- Schedule at least four hours of open time every week.

- Laugh every day and dance to your own beat

- Start every day by focusing on one part of your life for which you are most grateful.

- Wake up before the sun.

- Ask yourself throughout the day: "Is this the most important thing I should be doing right now?"

- Look at your upcoming week every Sunday night and evaluate if you are spending your time wisely.

- Do something kind for someone every day or give an honest compliment.

- Pause every hour to do three minutes of deep breathing without distraction.

- Release your stress and worries by brain-dumping daily to live an intentional life.

- Switched all of your bills to online billing and set them up on autopay when possible.

- Cleanse your car regularly and keep a bottle of essential oils on hand to drop in your car diffuser. My favorite is wild orange.

- Clean your house regularly, including organizing junk drawer(s), shelves, and clutter.

- Organize your closets regularly and create a stationary donation bag.

Exercise and Dietary Habits for Holistic Health

I was raised in a good environment that fostered good habits. When I was growing up, my parents made sure we had healthy food. They were also advocates for exercise and supported my considerable involvement in athletics. After I graduated college and started my own family, I worked out regularly during my lunch hour. I started focusing more on my eating habits during my first pregnancy, choosing to be more mindful of what I put into my body. As a result, I felt even stronger and more vibrant, and I had no pregnancy-related health concerns. I also decided when I awoke every morning that I would be mindful of my personal actions.

I've remained mindful of what I eat and how I exercise for ten years now because I've seen the benefits. My healthy choices in life provide me with a path toward being at my very best for my family. From the time I wake up to the time I go to bed, the way I care about myself makes a difference in how I am with others. If I weren't intentional about good health, I would be low on energy, short with my children, more forgetful, and not as responsive at work. I would be unable to compartmentalize my buckets because I would lack the desire to be intentional.

In other words, without physical and mental health, I'd be tired, grumpy, and frazzled.

Health in Community

Part of holistic health is being able to calm our thoughts. They can become very powerful and take us down a difficult path if we neglect to manage them. Having positive, good, clean thoughts keeps you strong. They will also help with your emotions.

Health is the foundation of happiness. Healthy people can handle their emotions. They can channel them correctly and accept them. They are more likely to implement change in their lives when change is needed. They are more likely to live at their best.

As a mom, you are your children's role model. From birth, you are the primary example they have in everything. If you are not healthy, if you are not approaching care for yourself, then they may not think that self-care is important. They may shrug it off and remove it from their own lives.

Your kids watch every decision you make. It's one of the main reasons to practice good, holistic health—so that you can show others how to be healthy.

There's this mentality in society that we have to do everything ourselves. Since the beginning of time, women were the ones who cared about the home. They came together and raised children, creating community for themselves and others.

But now we've created a culture in which we don't ask for help because we are ashamed to do so. We don't ask for "me time" because we don't think it's important. We don't focus on our mental and physical health because we can barely even keep up with the day's tasks.

The reason we can't do everything is because we feel like we have to do everything. Part of holistic health is asking for and accepting help. It's also offering that help to other people in need.

Let's become healthy communities again. Let's support one another and help one another succeed.

WORKBOOK

Chapter Seven Questions

Question: What healthy eating and living habits have you developed? Which areas need improvement? What areas of living a healthy lifestyle do you want to learn more about?

_____

_____

_____

_____

_____

_____

_____

_____

_____

_____

Question: What physical and emotional consequences do you notice when you neglect your health? What physical or emotional concerns do you have for your family's health, and how can you help them to manage those issues through healthy, holistic choices?

_____

_____

_____

_____

_____

_____

_____

_____

_____

_____

Journal: How can growing in a community increase your physical and mental health? Describe what it looks and feels like to belong to a community where each member is encouraging and helping the others and bringing out the best in one another.

Action: Attend a class, read a book, or watch a video

about an area of healthy living that is of interest and potential benefit to you and your family.

Chapter Seven Notes

CONCLUSION

Motivated by Love

In all of this growth and change there is one internal driver.

Love.

Happiness, contentment, fulfillment, achievement, emotional health, physical health—none of it is possible without love. Love for yourself and love for those around you.

You may not feel it right now. You may not feel very in love with yourself, and you may even be frustrated by others. But I ask you to open yourself up to it. Welcome it. Dare to let it rule your heart.

Because once love takes hold, everything will change.

You will know and understand self-care.

You will take control of your life.

You will be aware of your emotions.

You will change your response to your circumstances.

You will listen well.

You will connect with others.

You will manage your actions to accomplish your

goals.

We all lead busy lives, and I have written this book to show you that you can thrive instead of struggle. You can choose to be more mindful by making small, but important changes. You can transform your inner life in a powerful manner that will impact every aspect of your being. It has been my aim to give you small, manageable steps to become a person who practices mindfulness, leads a balanced life, and meets goals every time.

Self-care is a vital first step on the journey to a balanced life. We often get so busy taking care of others that we forget to look after our own health. Spending just a little time each day caring for yourself will pay huge dividends.

Practicing self-care means focusing on what is truly important and makes your life more meaningful and fulfilled. Self-care will look different for each person. A successful self-care routine will meet your fundamental needs and restore your energy, leading to an active and productive life, and creating healthy community.

I am a big proponent of a holistic approach to health, taking physical, emotional, and spiritual health into account. It is vitally important to cultivate healthy living habits that focus on eliminating toxins, managing stress, emphasizing joyful physical movement, and eating right for your body.

If you want to be healthy, you need to be able to calm yourself and manage your emotions. You also should learn to accept help from others, just like you support them. Accepting help isn't always easy, but it can make a big difference.

To achieve personal growth, you need to explore all your emotions, good and bad, and be present in them. Being in tune with your emotions will help you become emotionally mature. There are four steps to handling emotions: identifying when emotion is building within us, making a choice to deal with it, accepting it, and taking action. As you continue practicing mindfulness, you will learn to check in with yourself and successfully manage challenging situations.

You absolutely can take control of your own life, health, and mindset. Start owning your environment and making changes that allow you to love your life. Remember that you can only control your own actions, not those of other people.

The fact that you can't change or control others may be frustrating, but remember that you can always work on your own reactions. Come up with a strategy to start bringing about real change in yourself.

Active listening is a key strategy for a successful, fulfilled life, and it is something that takes effort. Solving problems between people requires active listening and patience, because change takes time. You can only learn from others if you approach them with an open mind and listen actively without judgment. Active listening will be beneficial in both your personal and professional life, so I highly recommend you take the time to try it.

As much as society tells you the opposite, it is important to learn to slow down and be intentional about how you spend your time. Overcommitment to outside activities is a serious problem that can be solved by slowing down.

Slowing down requires structure and the ability to be content with the mundane. Technology use can be a dangerous distraction and needs to be managed and limited. Make sure you focus your time on activities that are in line with your long-term goals. When you manage your actions, you take control of your life and make better use of your time. Managing your actions means being mindful of how you approach the things you have to do on a daily, weekly, or monthly basis. You have to be proactive and disciplined as you tackle projects. Moreover, you should be open to getting the help you need. Manage your actions so that you can focus on the things that matter and that enable you to lead a happy, fulfilled life guided by love.

Love is what will get you to the happiness that is possible in your life. So take that first step today. Take some time for you. Listen to a friend. Change your response to something in your life that is bothering you. All of these are ways to show love to yourself and others, and once you see that all of this is within your reach, nothing will be able to stop you.

APPENDIX

Recommended Reading

1. *The China Study: Revised and Expanded Edition* by T. Colin Campbell

2. *Whole Rethinking the Science of Nutrition* by T. Colin Campbell

3. *Cooked* by Michael Pollan

4. *The Omnivore's Dilemma* by Michael Pollan

5. *In Defense of Food* by Michael Pollan

6. *Selling Sickness* by Ray Moynihan

7. *The Miracle Morning for Network Marketers* by Hal Elrod

8. *The Power of Less* by Leo Babauta

9. *The Plant Paradox* by Dr. Gundry

10. *Himalayan Salt Crystal Lamps* by Clemence Lefevre

11. *Growing Up Mindful* by Christopher Willard

12. *Miss Minimalist* by Francine Jay

13. *The Blue Zones—9 Lessons for Living Longer from the People Who've Lived the Longest* by Dan Buettner

14. *Parenting Teens with Love and Logic* by Foster Cline, MD and Jim Fay

15. *Parenting with Love and Logic* by Foster Cline, MD and Jim Fay

16. *Revive* by Frank Lipman, MD

17. *No-Drama Discipline*, by Daniel J Siegel, MD and Tina Payne Bryson, PhD

18. *The Whole-Brain Child*, by Daniel J Siegel, MD and Tina Payne Bryson, PhD

19. *Brainstorm* by Daniel J Siegel, MD and Tina Payne Bryson, PhD

20. *A Still Quiet Place* by Amy Saltzman, MD

21. *Raising Happiness* by Christine Carter, PhD

22. *Buddha in Your Backpack* by Franz Metcalf

23. *Running with the Mind of Meditation* by Sakyong Mipham

24. *7 Habits of a Highly Effective Person* by Stephen Covey

25. *Listening Well the Art of Empathetic Understanding* by William R. Miller

26. *Buddhism for Mothers Series* (set of 3) by Sarah Naphtali

27. *Anti-Cancer—A New Way of Life* by Dr. David Serbian-Schreiber, MD, PhD

About the Author

Elizabeth Cook is a mother of six, wife, electrical engineering PhD student, full-time leader at an electric utility, partner in a family business, author, life coach, and avid book reader. Elizabeth is deeply dedicated to empowering people to live their fullest life.

With her approach to her and her family's health, she believes it is essential to care for your entire self and make intentional choices about what goes into, onto, and around your body while continuously checking on your mindset.

From her childhood upbringing, passion for books, and professional training at the Institute of Integrative Nutrition, where she studied a variety of theories and practical lifestyle coaching methods, she creates actionable road maps to move people toward their ideal visions of holistic health (emotional, physical, and spiritual). Elizabeth has a unique ability to challenge herself continuously with limited fear and enjoys creating environments of growth for those around her. Her company, Integrated Being, LLC, exists to provide people with the tools to make positive and lasting change in their lives.

When Elizabeth is not writing or creating space, you can find her scrambling to get the kids in the car for an adventure in the outdoors, enjoying a dark roast coffee on her front porch, or sitting still on her mat.

REFERENCES

Notes

[1] Seigel, Daniel J. and Tina Payne Bryson. *The Whole-Brain Child: 12 Revolutionary Strategies to Nurture Your Child's Developing Mind.* Random House, 2011.

[2] Torres, Monica. "Survey: Americans Reach a Record Level of Unhappiness." The Ladders. February 14, 2018. https://www.theladders.com/career-advice/survey-americans-reach-a-record-level-of-unhappiness.

[3] Hyman, Mark. "UltraMind®: Key #7 Calm Your Mind." Dr. Hyman. 2016. https://drhyman.com/blog/2010/08/24/the-ultramind-solution-key-7-calm-your-mind.

Made in the USA
Lexington, KY
05 December 2019

58200802R00068